CW00853479

1

From The Pink Sands

Away From The Stars

A gaze to the ocean

A ship sailing from the horizon

Lights illuminate the vessel

In the darkness of night

The early birds marching towards the land

As they chase the light away from the stars

My Summer of Love

Just like Lennon's 'Double Fantasy'

I'm embracing all that I know,

Experiencing the world with all its wonders;

On the devil's Isle

My soul will grow.

Fear of the unknown leaves most

Swimming in the shallows

A stone's throw away from

The place they were spat into the world.

Give me the deepest depths,

I'll show my ego

That it is okay to be answerless

I'll show my compass it is okay to be lost

I want my synapses firing on all cylinders

As I explore phenomena and horizons

Instead of creating monsters

To explain a quantum reality

Where most things lie on an arbitrary binary.

Start to see the beauty in mystery

Because even in tragedy

Lies a silver line of poetry,

If it's not already there-

Create it for yourself.

Remnants of wrecked ships greet the shores of

Bermuda

Amongst the marine life

Beyond the sands,

Are colourful houses in unique pastel shades

Their architecture can leave a shiver

In the midday sun

As you drink rum swizzles

Rubbing well-tanned shoulders

With the well-dressed locals

Sporting their blazers and Bermuda shorts.

Look past the bricks and mortar

And find the history;

See what the demons are trying to protect,

These rocks host the oldest church

In the western hemisphere,

The traditions give this visual paradise

More than just face value

Bermuda's culture runs deep,

Its pornographic landscapes and pink sands

Won the heart of Mark Twain

Who put the Devil's Isle above heaven;

I find it impossible to come back down again.

I know life isn't always a fairy tale

But if you never take the chance

And dance with the devil on his turf

What is your life truly worth?

What if I told you,

The ground that you are currently on

Can carry just as much beauty

Wherever you are

No matter how grey the sky

No matter how concrete the jungle.

Beauty is in the eye of the beholder

Now open wide.

Watch Hill Park

Nestled away next to John Smith's Bay,

Lies the geographical embodiment of peace.

You'll feel the stresses you carry decrease

And the wonders of the world come out to play.

It is visible when fleeting down the windy road,

Hidden when the eyes peek at the ocean,

The endless blanket of undulating bondi blue.

If you take a moment to sit on the rocks,

Close your eyes and get lost,

This is when you'll discover

This is the centre of the universe,

The physical channel to the astral plane.

Listening to the universe perorate,

Voices of wisdom to attain,

I snap back to the physical plane,

This physical vessel

With a calmness I maintain.

Spectating the endless ocean bed,

The sounds of calmly crashing waves

Against the rock face,

The present moment I embrace.

Moongates

I have mixed feelings on marriage

As much as I know it's a holy matrimony

At times a religious engagement of a

Couples unity

But is it not also just a legal binding?

Or an excuse to party

And open a joint bank account

Maybe if today's couples were married

Under moongates

They might have more luck

The Perfect Stranger

Restless in my tiny seat

I awaited our ascent into the air

When I got on this plane,

I was flying solo

But I couldn't help

Fixating on the woman next to me,

I couldn't help finding as much beauty in her

As I did in the sun above the clouds.

High on adrenaline

I watched the ground beneath me shrink

Tearing me away from my world

And turning the landscape beneath me

Into a cartoon comic strip.

We coasted through the clouds with ease

The sun shining

Into her blonde hair and blue eyes;

Small talk didn't feel so small with her.

The red wine started to flow

As we intoxicated each other

On anecdotes and stories

Until we hit the passport line

And went our separate ways.

No names.

Just a warm smile and a goodbye.

Memories of her will always leave me on a high.

No matter how transitory

I'm glad she became a fleeting part of my story.

Tree Sitting

Gazing upon a spectacular display of objects,

It is not what the eye can see

That is needed to capture this.

Upon its arrival,

A glowing creation.

The mind thrived to create such a thing,

Leaving behind vibrant emotion.

The lingering sense of self,

Present.

It is neither what was before,

Or shall be,

This is infinite.

For it is not the illusion

In which we conjure,

But only a print of the soul.

Let go of all known wrong,

Feel the mark of nature's song.

Capture the moment,

Let it unfold.

Behold,

This is the sight of light.

Um-Um

The long tail soared through the saltwater air,

Gombays stomped,

Spinned,

Twisted

And whistled

As Bermuda's spectators stopped and stared.

The locals turned to each other and mumbled

"Um-Um dat little bie be micing".

Pointing at the flamboyantly dressed child.

"Bet his mama won't let him go diving".

Laughing,

They turned towards each other and smiled.

Tourists dive from cliffs,

Into the bluest of oceans.

Toe gaps filled with pink sand,

Drinking rum swizzles.

Beach bums sipping booze,

Applying lotion

But the sun came out with a slight drizzle.

Lizards dancing on hibiscus flowers,

Those reptilians must have superpowers.

Particles

The breezy force brushes and paints my face

With the tones of the ancients

Placed on limestone at Astwood park

Emitting frequencies and allowing us to perceive

Total relief as all tensions lessen

Our bodies reduce to particles

As we become one with the environment

Shorelines and gusts of wind greet us

To the world beyond our sight

As we transcend and become meer dust

Off we go on an adventure

A journey to nothing

As we close our eyes and subside

Wave goodbye to the worries of this life

Close your eyes and wave goodbye

Relinquishing all known

New Day

Polar opposites combine

A reaction so divine

The sun and the moon

Leave symbols and runes

That map out our storyline

Floating in cloud nine

Solar and lunar forces align

Crashing waves

Upon ancient graves

That forge our pink shoreline

A peek of sunshine

Giving us a sign

That night has become day

In this beautiful way

Where the moon recedes

And the sun provides

Light to come out and play

Goleuo

My vision crystalline as I open my eyes at the
crack of dawn,
Scratching away at the sleep surrounding my
eyelids,
A good indication of a peacefully deep slumber

My skin shed because today's a new day,
I stretch and manoeuvre out of the sheets.
Today I'm feeling glad,
Today I will what do makes me happy
And today I'm not worrying about the
consequences

It is said,

Do what thou wilt,

But do not do what affects others.

So if that is at the core of our instinctual

actions,

Why are we ever swayed from our happiness?

Today I'm helping others,

Today is about community

And today I'm not worrying

About anything other than commemorating

And sharing the pleasures of existence

There will be some who challenge your glow.

Don't you worry about artificial smiles,

Under no obligation

Do you have to push false positivity on them

Because bears don't even eat porridge.

Nothing is a straight line,

But a spiral.

Island of Devils

The isle of devils

Surrounded by shipwrecks

Populated by pigs

Destined to impress

In modern day

There's windy streets

And crooked lanes

Reckless drivers

Bikes weaving traffic

Imagine the disdain

Parrot fish glow under the bridge

Swimming in coordinated rotations

Old railway trails

Bring light to bermuda's hidden wonders

What was once mobile transportation

Has become a favourited walking trail

Bringing light to natural detail

The place where mould grows fast

Metals rust quick

The place where things don't last

Printed in Great Britain
by Amazon